SIGN LANGUAGE
FOR BABIES AND TODDLERS

Children's Reading & Writing Education Books

All Rights reserved. No part of this book may be reproduced or used in any way or form or by any means whether electronic or mechanical, this means that you cannot record or photocopy any material ideas or tips that are provided in this book.

Copyright 2016

Sign Language is one way of communicating with young kids through actions and gestures of the hands and body.

EAT

DRINK

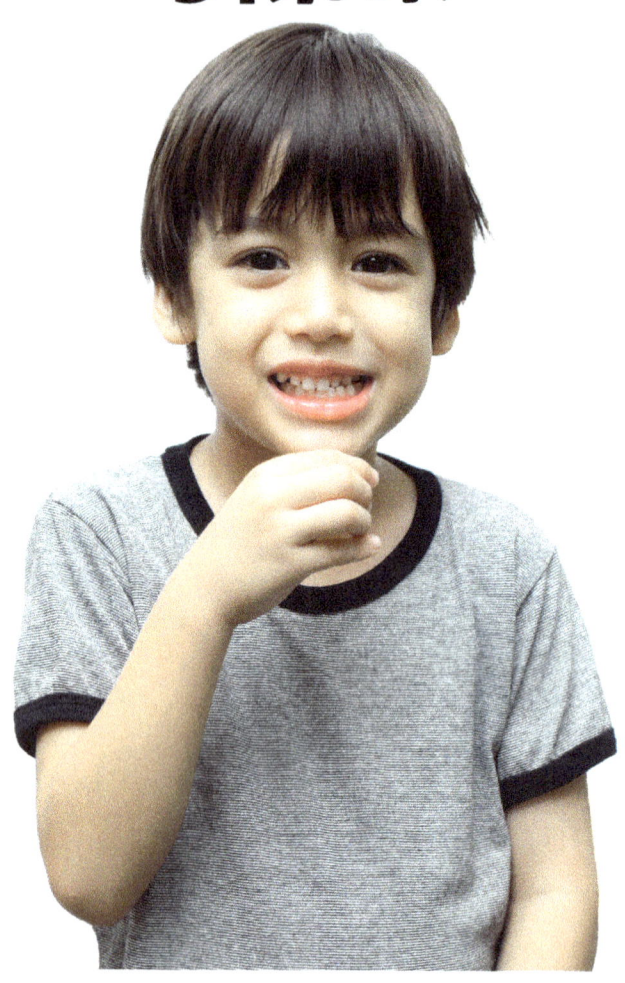

MORE

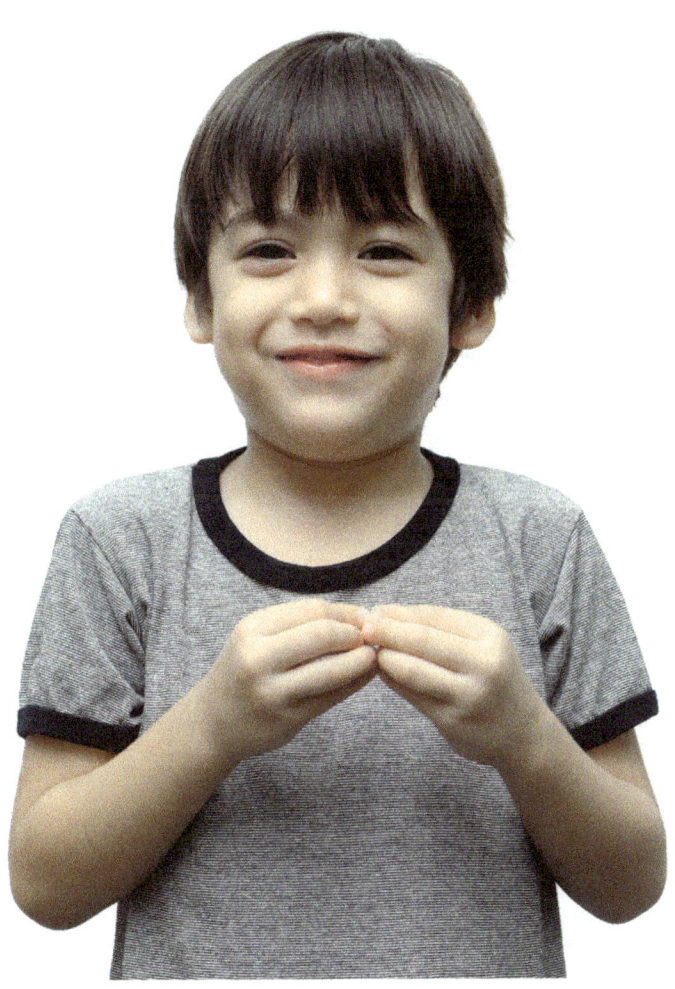

PLEASE

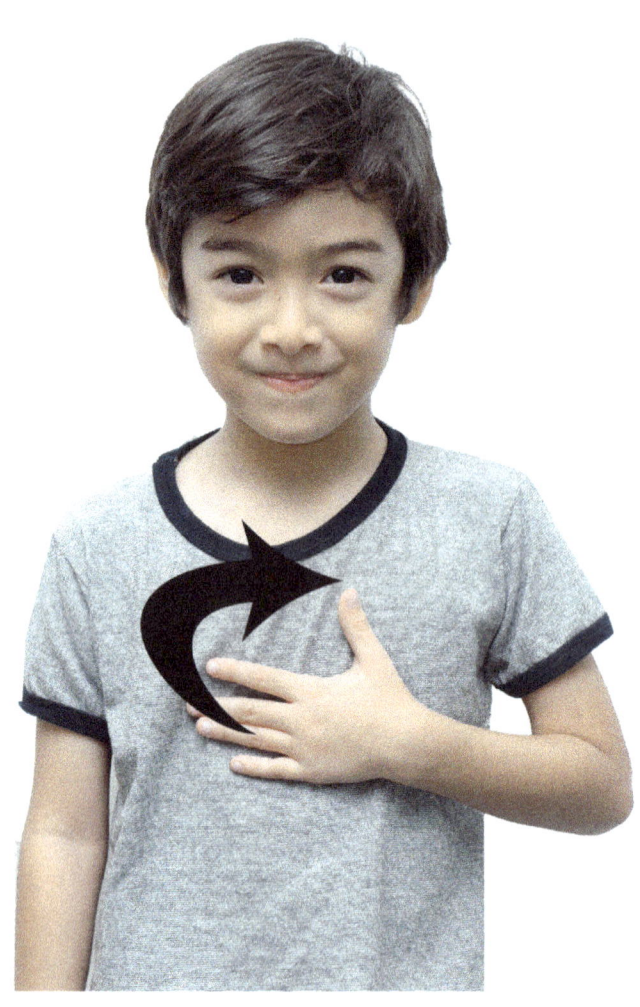

THANK YOU

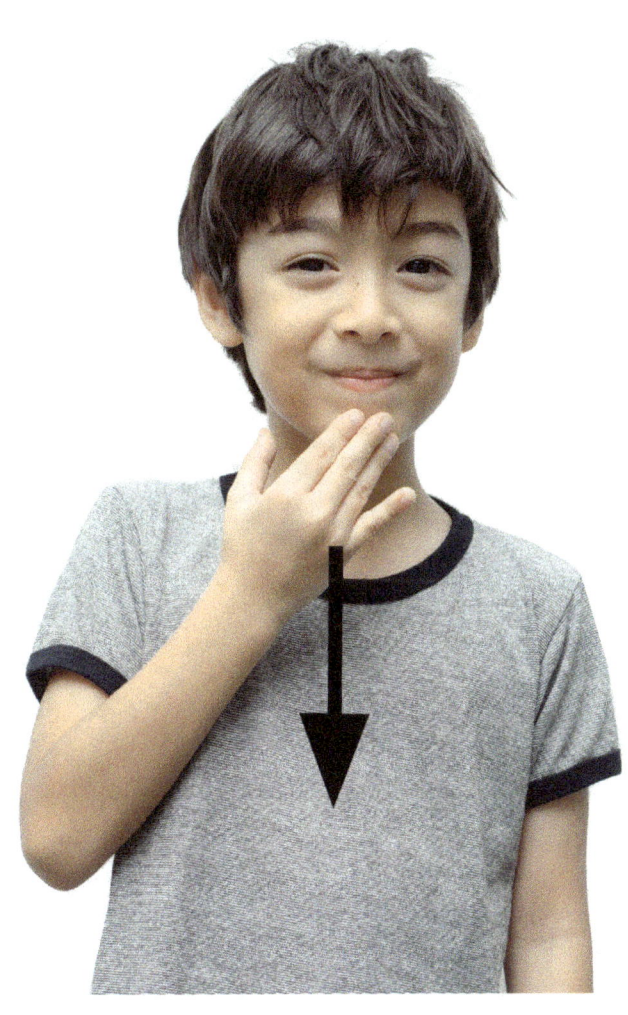

SORRY

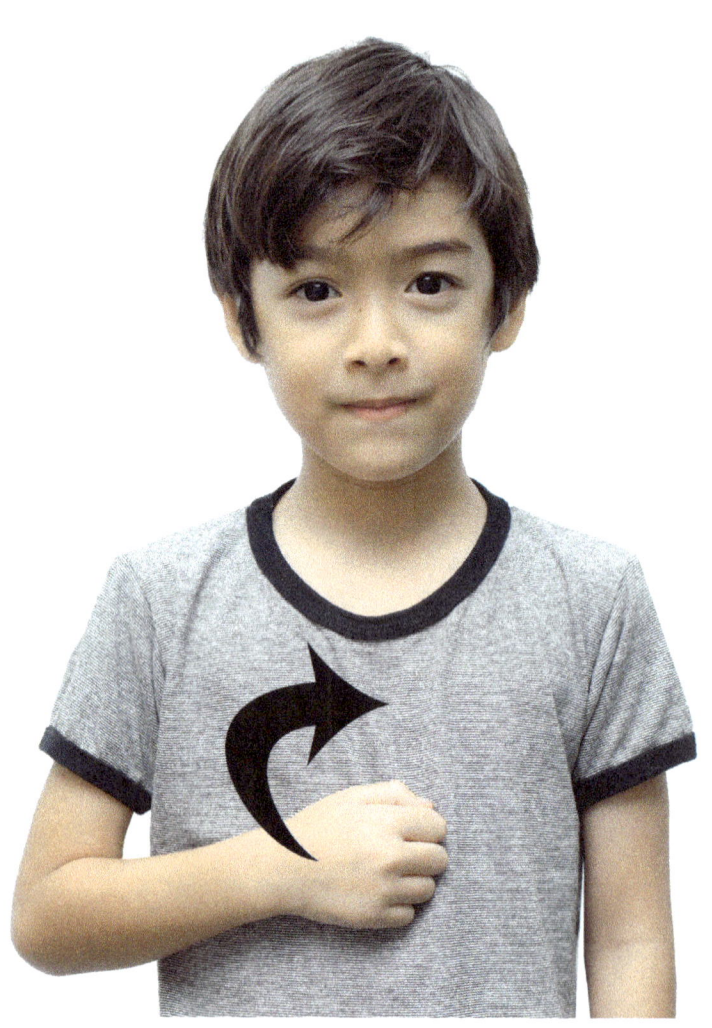

RED

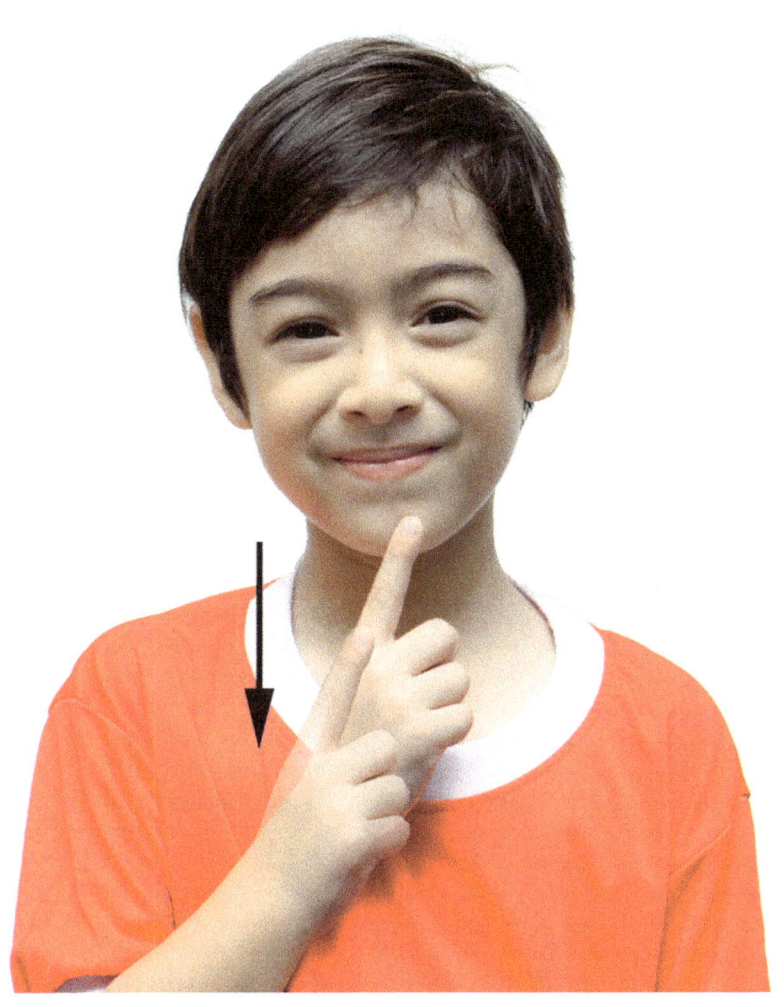

ORANGE

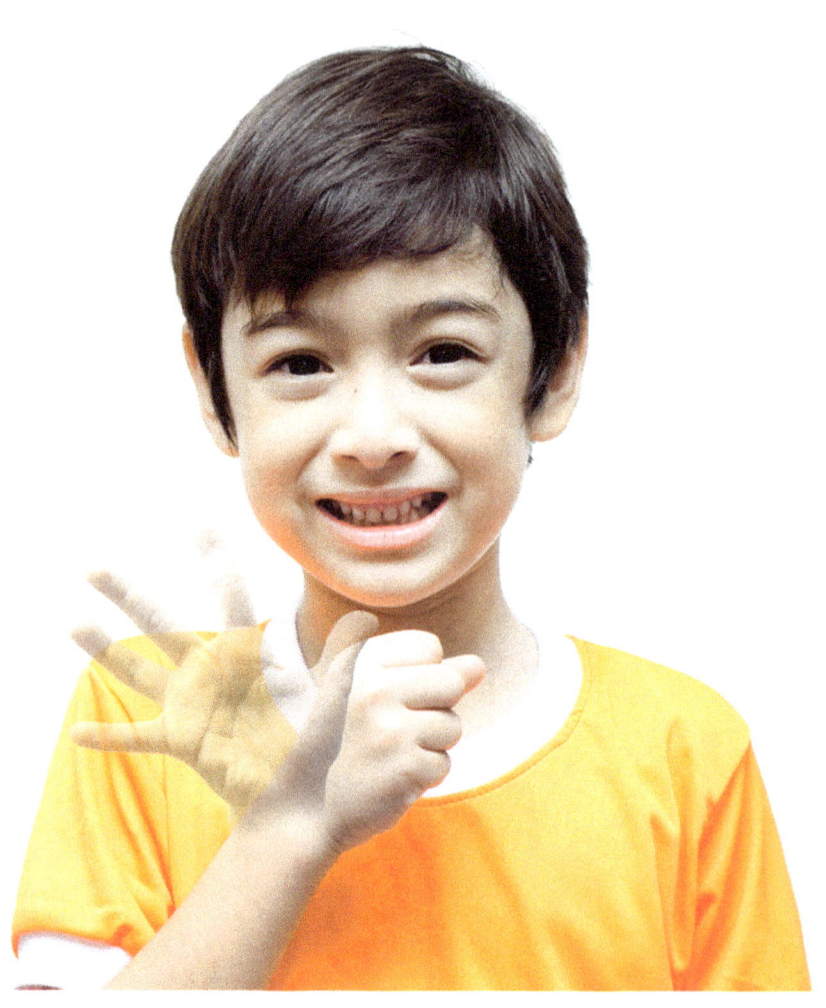

YELLOW

GREEN

PURPLE

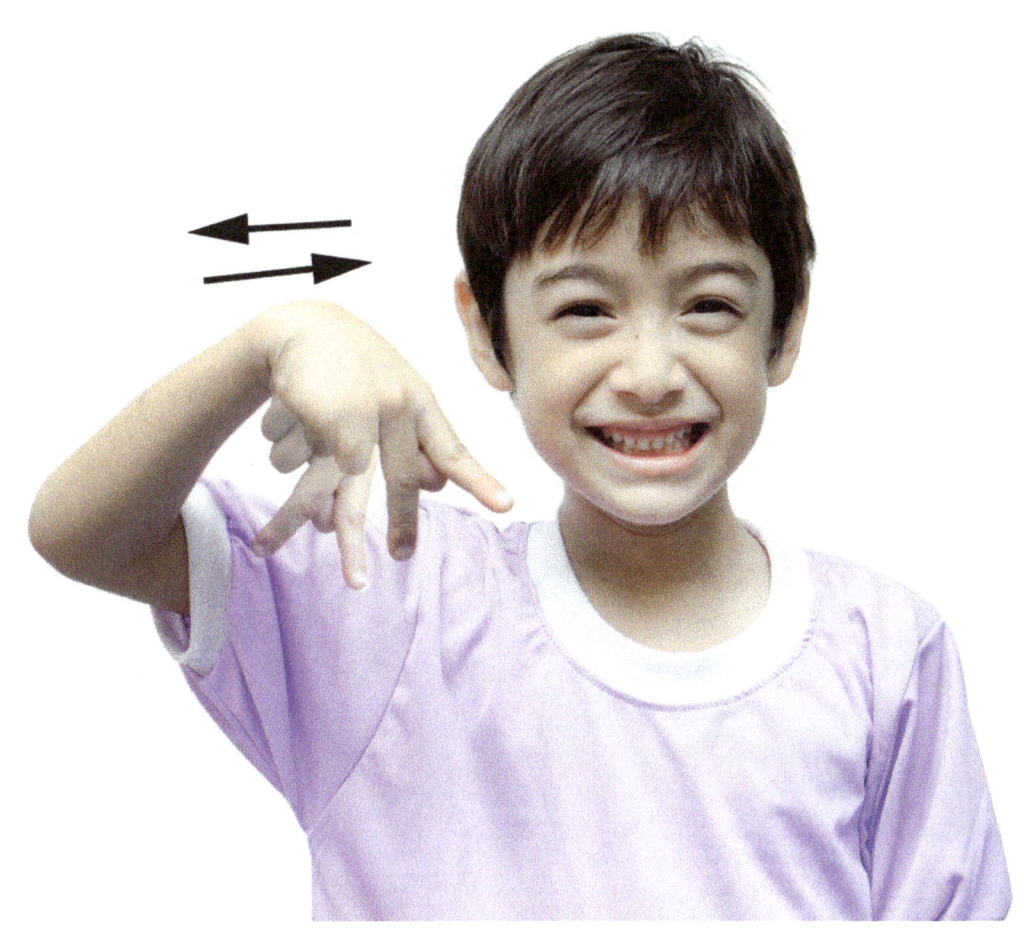

BLUE

BAD

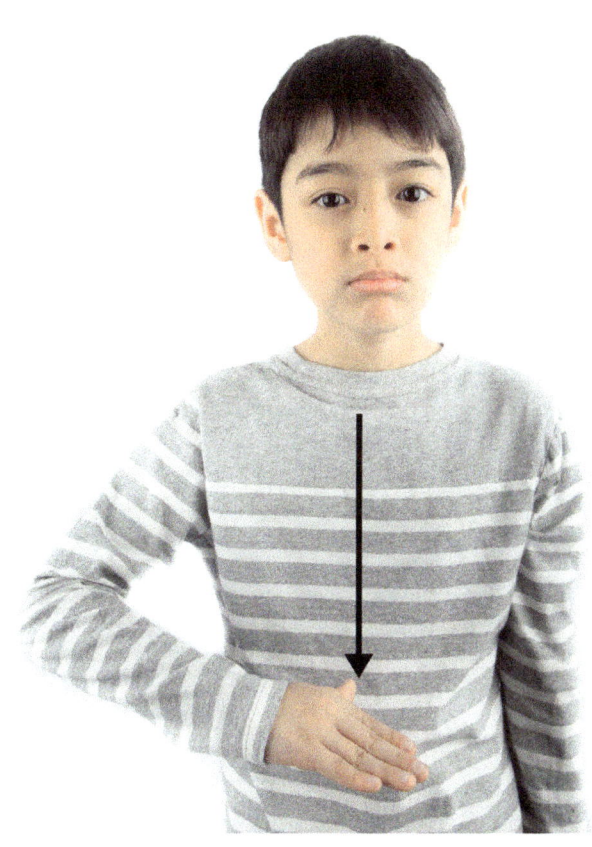

GOOD

BETTER

BEST

SUN

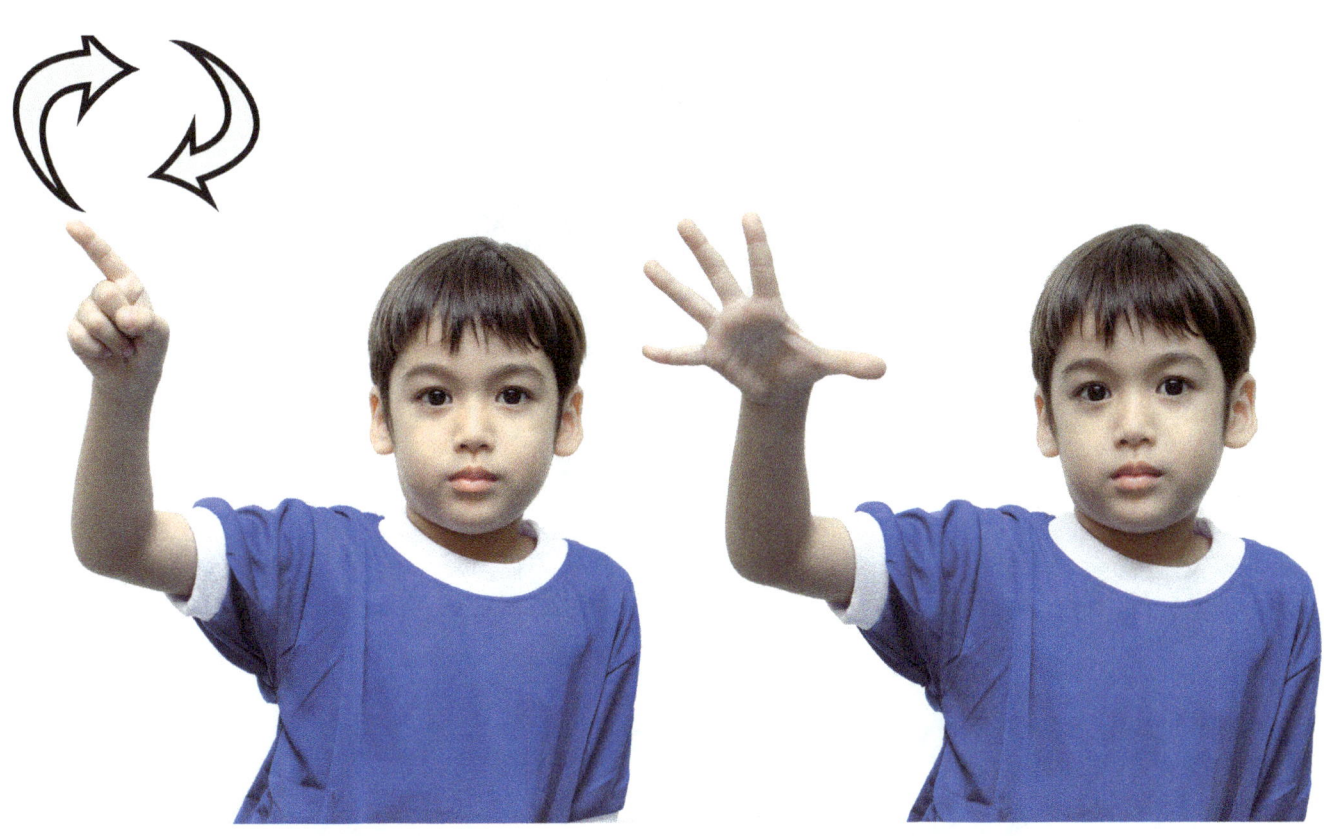

STOP

SILLY

GRUMPY

WORST

SICK

PRAY

Basic hand Sign Language

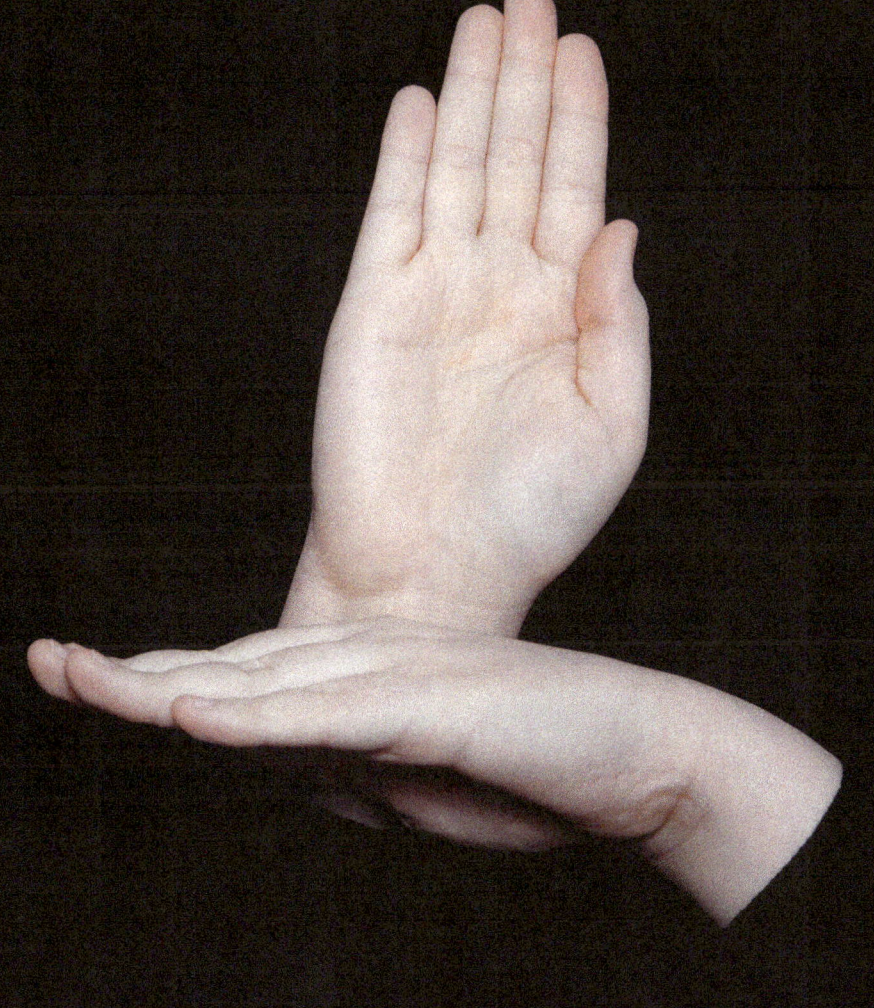

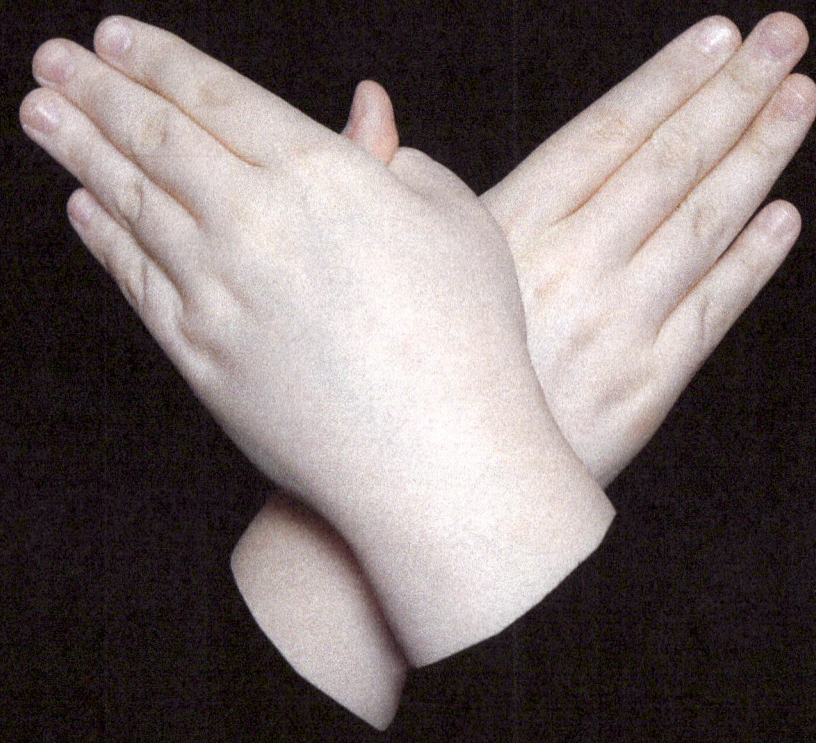

BUTTERFLY

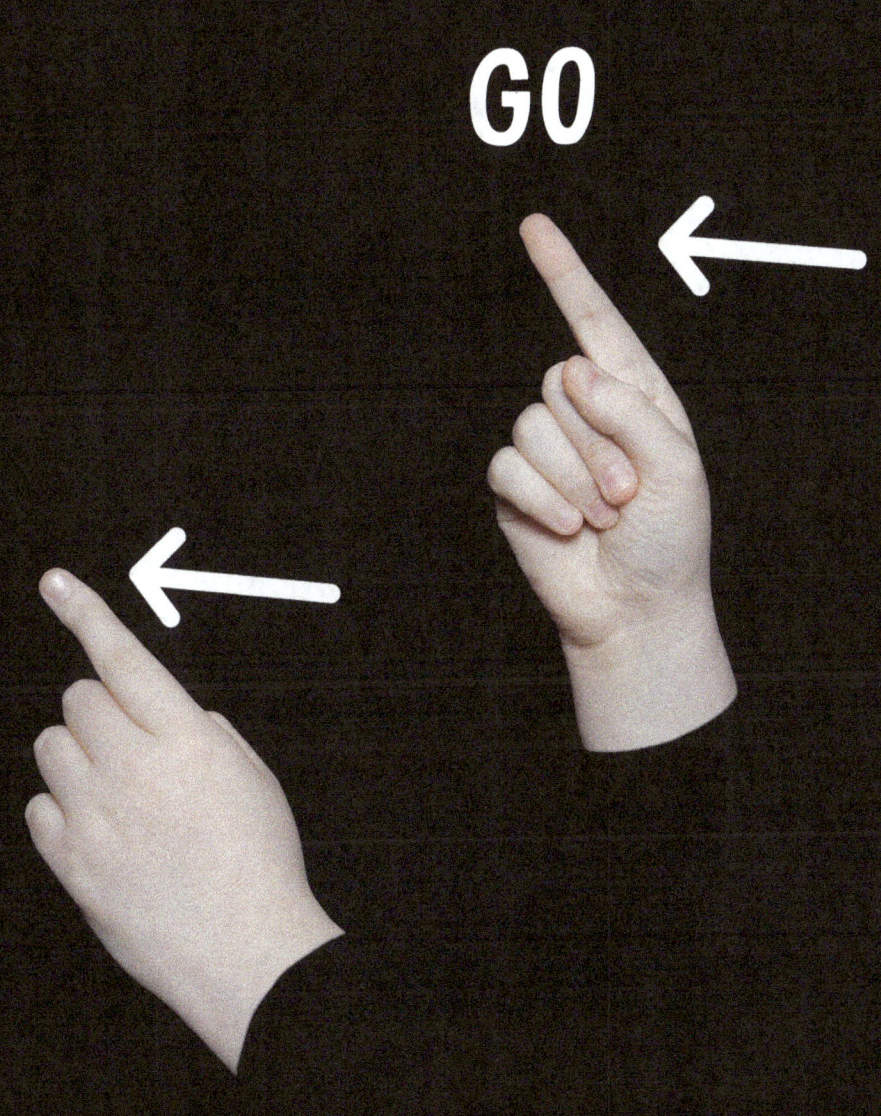

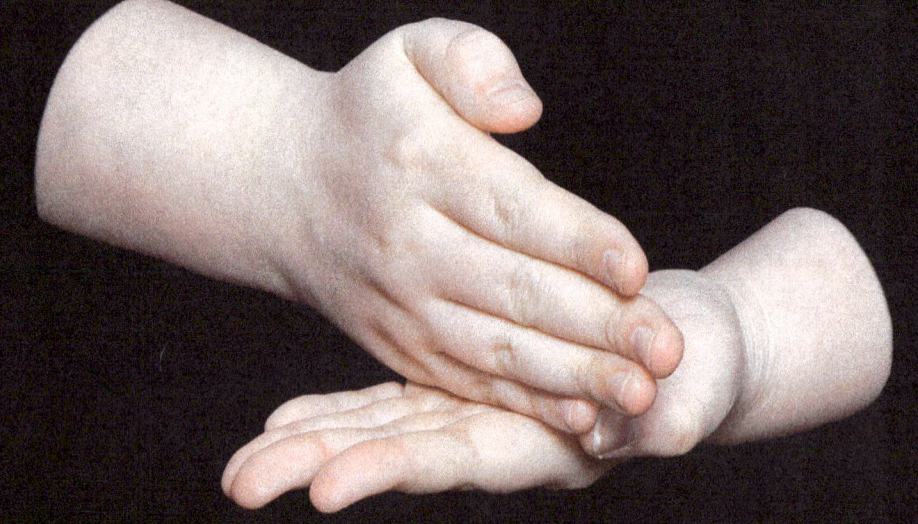

THAT

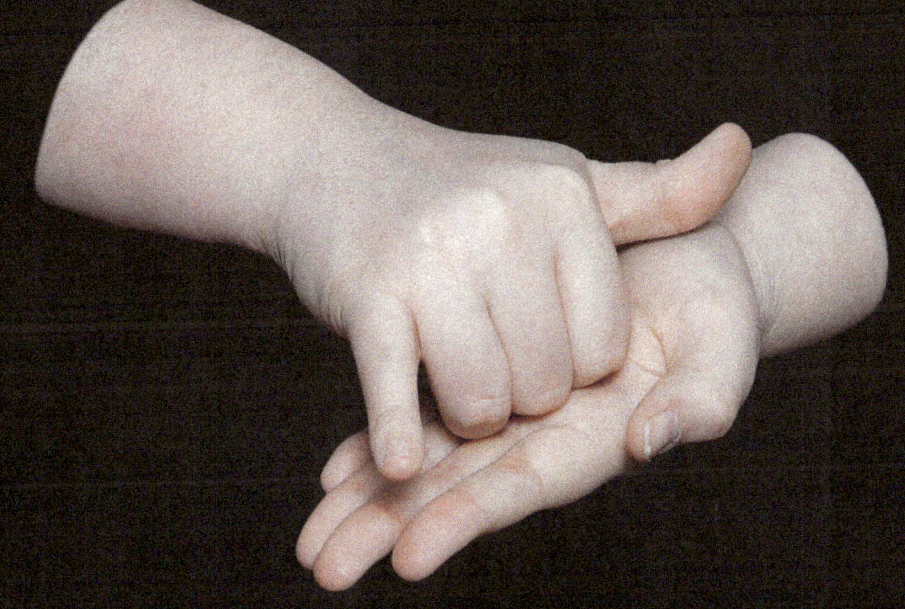

MILK

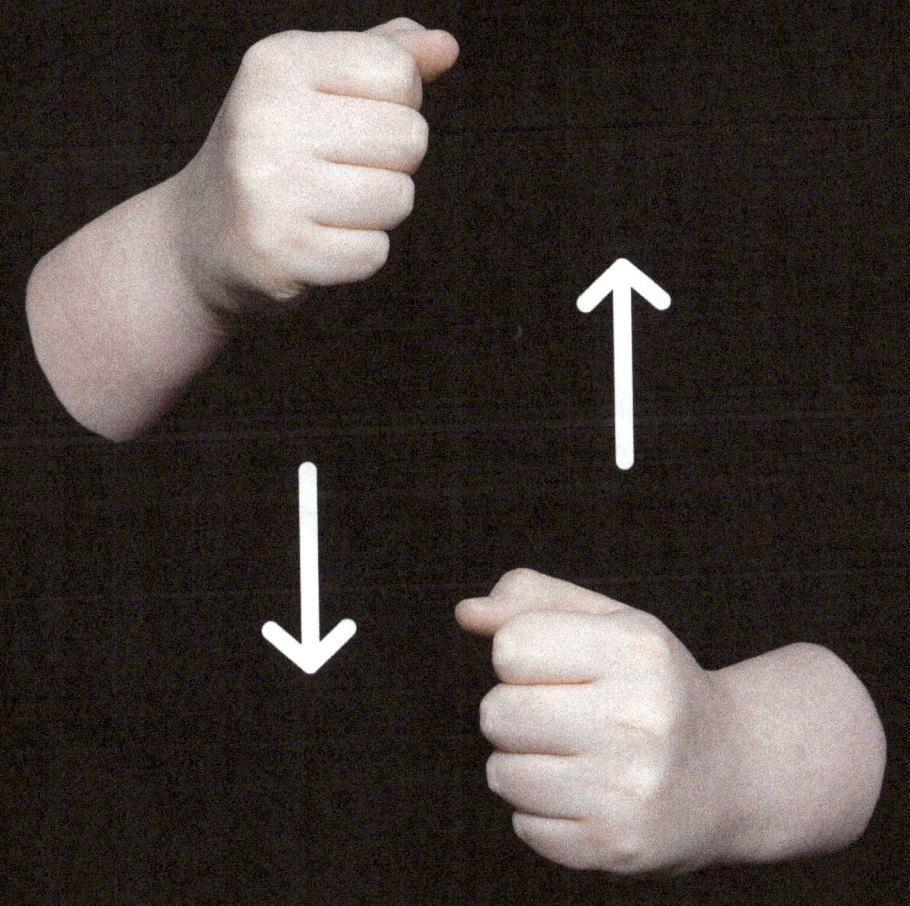

FRIEND

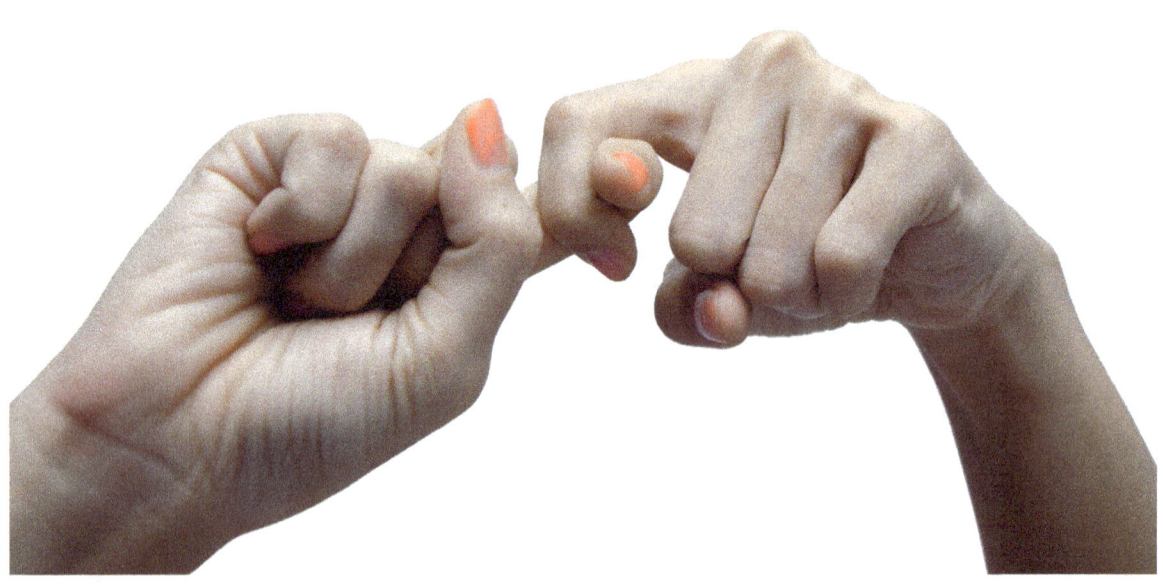

HELP

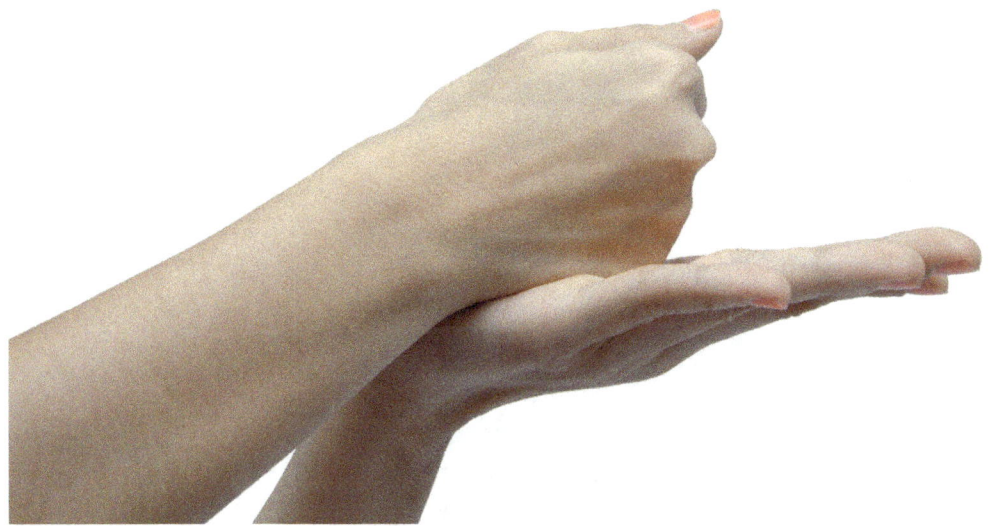

SAME

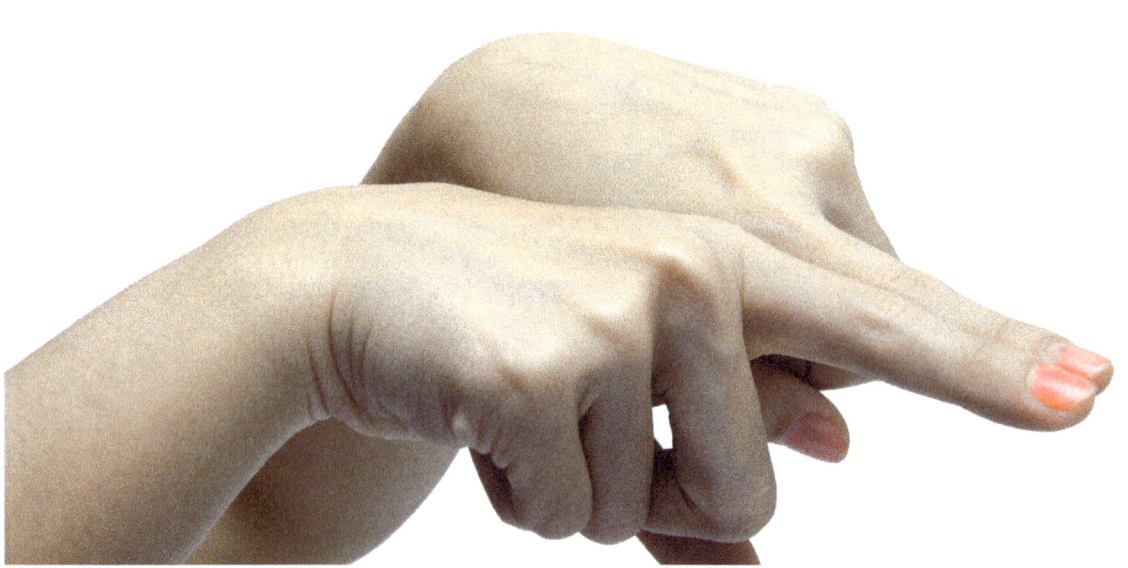

TIME

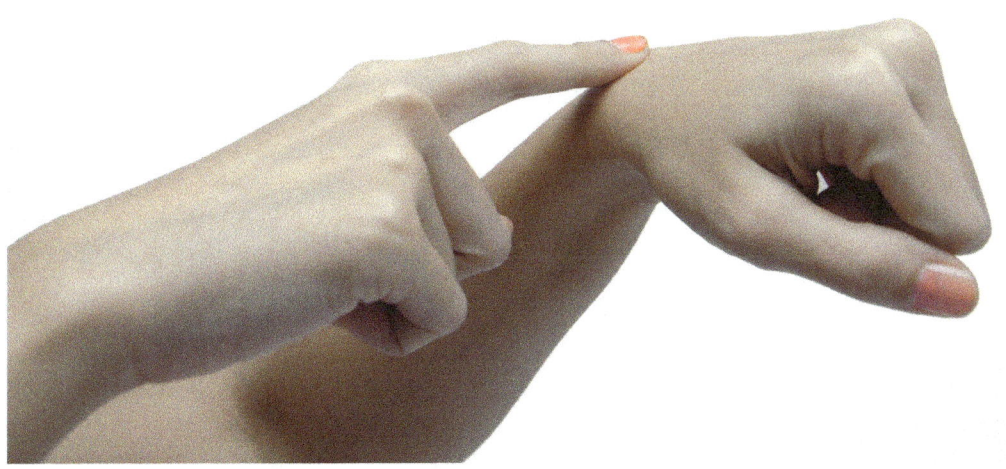

www.ingramcontent.com/pod-product-compliance
Lightning Source LLC
LaVergne TN
LVHW082254070426
835507LV00037B/2290